The Weapons of World War II

PETER BENOIT

Children's Press®
An Imprint of Scholastic Inc.
New York   Toronto   London   Auckland   Sydney
Mexico City   New Delhi   Hong Kong
Danbury, Connecticut

Content Consultant

James Marten, PhD
Professor and Chair, History Department
Marquette University, Milwaukee, Wisconsin

Library of Congress Cataloging-in-Publication Data
Benoit, Peter, 1955–
The Weapons of World War II / by Peter Benoit.
    pages cm. — (A true book)
Includes bibliographical references and index.
ISBN 978-0-531-20495-5 (library binding) — ISBN 978-0-531-21730-6 (paperback)
1. World War, 1939–1945—Juvenile literature. 2. Weapons—Juvenile literature. I. Title.
D743.7.B467 2014
940.54'2—dc23   2014003937

All rights reserved. Published in 2015 by Children's Press, an imprint of Scholastic Inc.
Printed in the United States of America 113
SCHOLASTIC, CHILDREN'S PRESS, A TRUE BOOK™, and associated logos are trademarks and/or
registered trademarks of Scholastic Inc.

1 2 3 4 5 6 7 8 9 10 R 24 23 22 21 20 19 18 17 16 15

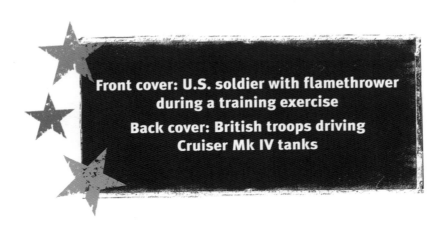

Front cover: U.S. soldier with flamethrower
during a training exercise

Back cover: British troops driving
Cruiser Mk IV tanks

Find the Truth!

Everything you are about to read is true *except* for one of the sentences on this page.

Which one is **TRUE**?

T or F   Some land mines used in World War II launched into the air before exploding.

T or F   British researchers never cracked Germany's secret code during World War II.

Find the answers in this book.

H.1 -45

Contents

THE **BIG** TRUTH!

Technology and War

The word *grenade*
comes from the French
word for pomegranate.

Soldiers make their way toward Normandy, France.

3 War at Sea

4 Destruction!

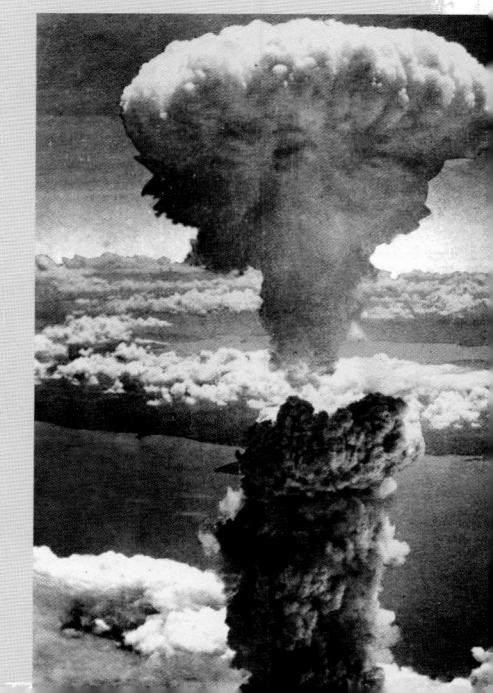

The United States dropped an atomic bomb on Nagasaki, Japan, on August 9, 1945.

5

A British biplane (foreground) chases down a German plane during World War I.

War in the Heavens

In wartime, when one country invents a new weapon, other countries find ways to copy it, improve it, or protect themselves from it. The competition leads to huge changes in a very short time. For example, airplanes were widely used in warfare for the first time in World War I (1914–1918). Over the course of the war, metal planes replaced wood-and-canvas ones. **Engineers** developed ways to shoot guns and drop bombs. After World War II began in 1939, the technology advanced even more.

A dogfight is a battle between warplanes.

Bomber Planes

Bombers are specialized planes built to carry bombs. During World War II, engineers worked to design bombers that would carry heavier explosives for greater distances and drop them more accurately. Some designs were more successful than others. Germany's Heinkel He 177 Greif (Griffin) bomber was nicknamed the Torch because its engines often caught fire. However, this did not mean Torches were not powerful. Later models could carry more than 6.5 tons of explosives.

Workers check and refuel a Heinkel He 177.

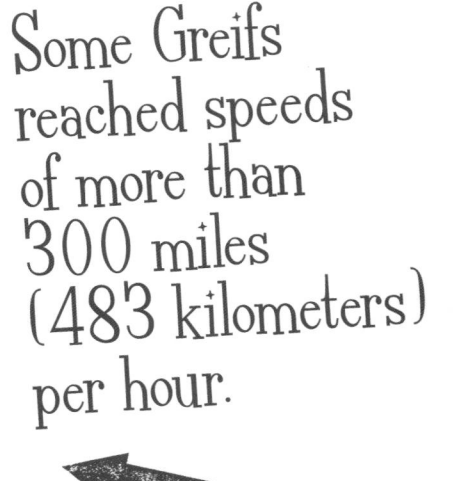

Some Greifs reached speeds of more than 300 miles (483 kilometers) per hour.

A Stuka drops bombs as it dives near the ground.

Germany's Stuka bombers were generally more successful than the Greifs. These dive-bombers could aim very accurately. They led the way in Adolf Hitler's 1939 swift, effective **blitzkrieg** on Poland. Stukas had screaming sirens that terrified civilians. However, early Stukas were slow and carried a small load. The Stuka was eventually redesigned, and large guns called cannons were added.

A Hurricane patrols over Britain.

Hurricanes and Spitfires

Fighter planes also played a major role in the war. These planes were small, fast, and built to shoot down enemy aircraft. They flew alongside bombers to protect them. During the Battle of Britain in 1940, the German air force, or Luftwaffe, attacked targets in Britain. German Messerschmitt fighters came up against Britain's Hurricanes and Spitfires. These British planes were an enormous challenge for the German fighters to combat.

Hurricanes did most of the work against the German bombers. Hurricanes were durable, which means they were hard to destroy. They also carried more weapons than the Spitfires carried. The Spitfire was a more agile fighter than the Hurricane. It had thin, oval wings and could turn quickly and easily. Spitfires focused on shooting down the German fighters that guarded the bombers. The effectiveness of the British fighter planes eventually proved too much for the Luftwaffe. Germany called off its invasion of Britain.

Britain lost 1,012 aircraft during the Battle of Britain. Germany lost 1,918.

Spitfires were made to be agile at low altitudes, or lower to the ground.

Devastators and Avengers

Planes took to the sea during World War II. Some aircraft were designed to take off from and land on large ships called aircraft carriers. The U.S. Navy's Devastator was a **torpedo** bomber built to attack enemy ships. It had already been around for four years by the time the United States entered the war in 1941, but it had trouble competing with other warplanes. It was slow and not very agile.

Devastators fly over Hawaii in early 1941. By the end of the year, U.S. military planes were painted gray or green.

An Avenger comes in to land on the deck of an aircraft carrier.

Carrier ships had hooks to catch a plane as it landed.

The U.S. Navy responded by introducing a new torpedo bomber, the Avenger. During the course of the war, the Avenger became a powerful weapon. It could carry four 500-pound (227-kilogram) bombs. On board, it had **radar** to track enemy planes and ships. The Avenger also had special devices to trick the enemy's radar. Avengers were effective at attacking Japanese battleships and protecting U.S. ships.

CHAPTER 2

Land Attack!

Engineers spent World War I improving land weapons, too. Guns were made bigger and faster and were able to shoot longer distances. Tanks made powerful guns mobile. These vehicles were built with heavy armor for protection, making them difficult to destroy. During World War II, these technologies were improved further. One German machine gun, the MG42, was so effective it is still in widespread use today.

The MG42 was nicknamed Hitler's Buzzsaw, because of the sound of its rapid series of shots.

Soviet T-34 tanks enter Prague, Czechoslovakia, in 1945.

Tanks

Tanks were important during World War II. From the beginning, these weapons played a central role in Germany's battle **strategy**. German Panzer tanks were used together in a large group. They were almost unbeatable at first. Soviet engineers developed the T-34, first used against the Germans in 1941. It had thick, rounded armor that was tough to destroy. By 1943, it was effectively driving the Germans out of the Soviet Union.

The first U.S. tanks used in the war were far behind existing tank technology. Then, in 1942, U.S. engineers produced the M4 Sherman. The Sherman was less powerful and durable than other tanks, but it was faster. Germany responded by creating Panthers and Tigers. These tanks were slower than the Sherman. However, they were more durable and accurate. Late in the war, the Allies added things such as flamethrowers to help the Sherman compete with German tanks.

A Sherman tank races through the desert in Tunisia.

Bazookas and Panzerschreck

Both sides in the war developed ways to fight against enemy tanks. Rocket-powered weapons such as the American bazooka fired explosive **ammunition** that could pierce through the outside of a tank. One type of ammunition created a shock wave in the tank's armor. This caused chunks of the metal interior to explode. This kind of ammunition was occasionally fired at buildings. Another type of ammunition created plumes of hot, thick smoke.

A U.S. soldier demonstrates how to fire a bazooka.

18

Panzerschreck means "tank fright" in German.

The first bazookas were used by U.S. troops in North Africa in 1942. German soldiers captured some of the bazookas. German engineers used these examples to develop an even more powerful weapon, the Panzerschreck. The Panzerschreck fired a rocket that could pass through around 8 inches (20 centimeters) of armor. Many tanks were only half that thick. As the war progressed, tanks were built with thicker armor, and bazookas were made more powerful to attack them.

Soldiers on the British coast load a Bofors gun with ammunition.

Bigger and Better

Antiaircraft guns were built to shoot down aircraft from the ground. Multiple countries developed such guns. One of the most common among the Allies was the Swedish-built Bofors gun. Britain's Royal Navy adapted the Bofors gun for battles at sea. Similar guns were placed outside of London in Britain. In Germany, antiaircraft guns mounted to concrete towers protected the capital of Berlin from air attacks.

Katyusha

The Soviet Union's Katyusha rocket launcher
combined power with mobility. The Katyusha could
fire several rockets at the same time. These rockets
could be fired at targets 3 miles (5 km) away. The
Katyusha's largest ammunition weighed 64 pounds
(29 kg). This weapon could be moved on a truck
or a trailer. Being mobile helped protect the rocket
launcher. After it was fired, it could be moved
before enemy soldiers could fight back and try to
destroy it. Katyushas were less accurate than the
Bofors gun but more destructive.

Buried Weapons

Land mines were widely used during World War II. Buried just beneath the surface of the ground, mines exploded when tanks or soldiers passed over them. One of the most deadly German land mines was called the Bouncing Betty. When it was walked on, the mine would launch 3 feet (1 meter) into the air. There, it exploded, throwing **shrapnel** in all directions. To protect themselves, U.S. forces used a Bangalore torpedo. This device cleared a path through minefields.

Germany produced almost two million Bouncing Betties during World War II.

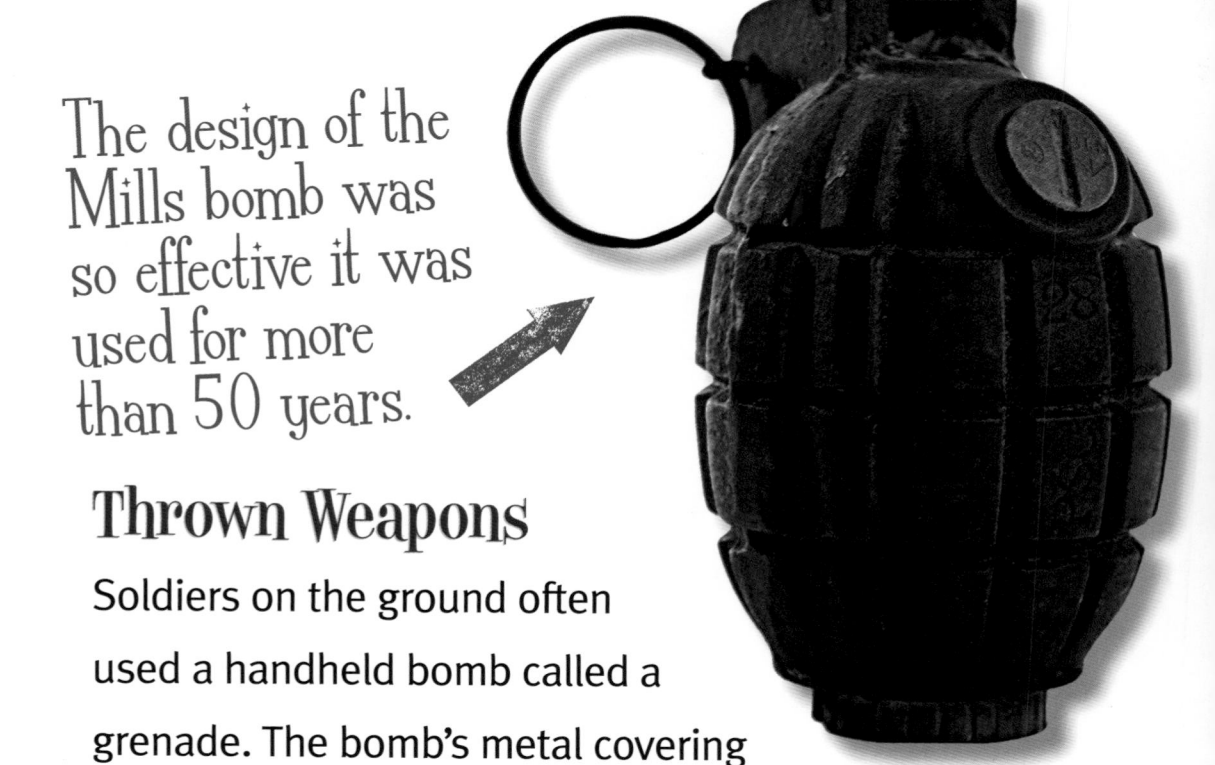

The design of the Mills bomb was so effective it was used for more than 50 years.

Thrown Weapons

Soldiers on the ground often used a handheld bomb called a grenade. The bomb's metal covering broke apart when it exploded, hurling shrapnel. Some early grenades were dangerous for the thrower. They could easily blow up before they were supposed to. From 1915 and into World War II, the British Mills bomb was revolutionary in its safety features. It included a safety lever and a pin that together worked in such a way that the grenade could only blow up after it was thrown.

Technology and War

Not all World War II technology was focused on destruction. Some very important inventions helped communicate information. Certain technologies helped troops locate the enemy or provided warnings before an attack. Other developments helped protect or reveal secret plans.

Sonar is a technology that was first developed during World War I. It was improved and widely used in World War II. Sonar allowed ships to locate targets, torpedoes, and other ships in the water.

On land, radar helped detect approaching planes. The early warning allowed British citizens and the Royal Air Force (RAF) to prepare for bomber attacks. This helped during the Battle of Britain and the bombing of London. Radar was also used at sea.

Militaries communicated using codes so the enemy could not understand their plans. The Germans used a machine called Enigma. It automatically coded messages as they were typed. It made communication fast and easy. It was also almost impossible for an enemy to decode—but only almost. Polish experts partially cracked the code in 1932, and British researchers decoded it further in 1940.

British battleships patrolled
the northern oceans for the new
German U-boats during World War I.

CHAPTER 3

War at Sea

War had taken place at sea for centuries before World War II. Over the years, metal ships had replaced wooden ones. Guns used at sea became more powerful, more accurate, and easier to use. Ships were even developed to move deep under the ocean. In addition, changes made to the weapons used in the air and on land often affected the weapons used on the water.

The North Sea was filled with both German and British sea mines during World War I.

Underwater Warfare

During both world wars, Germany was known for its submarines, called U-boats. Throughout World War II, U-boats patrolled the Atlantic Ocean. There, they disrupted U.S. shipments of food and supplies to Britain. U-boats patrolled in groups called wolf packs. These teams surrounded a ship and destroyed it. The United States and its allies had difficulty protecting their ships over such a large area. By the war's end, U-boats had sunk more than 2,800 U.S. shipping vessels.

"U-boat" in German is *U-boot*. This is short for *Unterseeboot*, which means "undersea boat."

28

Torpedoes could be launched from above or below the water.

Submarines and other ships often used underwater weapons called torpedoes. The earliest torpedoes were very unreliable. Occasionally, German torpedoes accidentally sank other U-boats in a wolf pack. By 1942, Germany developed better torpedoes that steered toward loud noises. The U.S. Navy created decoys that made noise to distract the torpedoes and lead them away from U.S. ships.

Some airplanes' wings could be folded up to take up less room on a carrier.

Aircraft Carriers

World War II fighter planes could fly no more than 1,200 miles (1,931 km) before having to refuel. Engineers around the world solved this problem by building huge ships called aircraft carriers. Carriers transported fighter planes across the ocean. The planes could land on or take off from a carrier's long, flat top called the flight deck. The largest U.S. carriers were called Essex class. They were 888 feet (271 m) long with massive flight decks.

Pearl Harbor

Japan's attack on Pearl Harbor in Hawaii in December 1941 brought the United States into World War II. It also highlighted how important aircraft carriers could be in war. The Japanese navy had used six aircraft carriers in the attack. From their decks, 350 bombers had taken off in two waves to attack the Pearl Harbor naval base. The attack sank or damaged 21 U.S. ships and destroyed nearly 200 U.S. aircraft.

Destroyers and Landing Craft

Destroyers were general-purpose ships. They often worked together to guard larger ships transporting troops and supplies. However, they were built for the heat of combat. They fought aircraft and submarines. They torpedoed enemy ships, sometimes taking on much larger battleships. Destroyers were commonly used to place underwater mines outside enemy harbors. Many of their duties were very dangerous, and destroyers and their crews often sank in battle.

Sailors lower an underwater mine into the ocean.

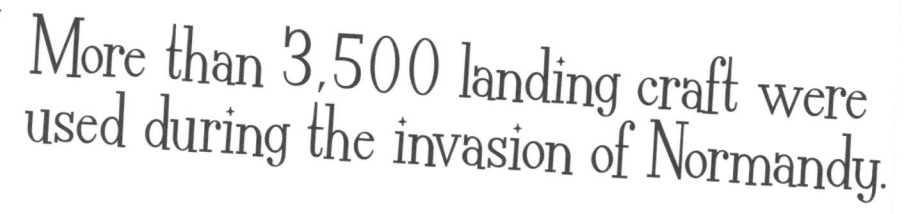

More than 3,500 landing craft were used during the invasion of Normandy.

Destroyers also shot at beaches to protect troops going ashore. A type of vehicle called a landing craft was developed specifically to carry troops ashore during such invasions. The smallest landing craft were lowered from larger ships. They carried a few dozen soldiers. Larger landing craft carried up to 200 people, as well as jeeps, small tanks, and supplies. Landing craft played an important role in the June 1944 D-Day invasion of Normandy in France.

A police officer offers tea to a bombing survivor in London, England.

Destruction!

World War II technology changed the postwar world. Some of the war's most destructive weapons made war seem deadlier and more impersonal than ever. Other new weapons were based on familiar ideas but stretched them to the limits of imagination. Enormous cannons, radio-controlled bombs, and atomic bombs marked new frontiers. Though used less often, these weapons magnified the horrors of war for both soldiers and civilians.

World War II rocket weapons helped lead to space exploration technology.

British nicknames for the German V1 included the doodlebug and the buzz bomb.

RAF pilots would "tip" V1s off course by nudging the bomb's wings while in flight.

V-Weapons

In June 1944, Germany first used its new Vergeltungswaffen 1, or V1 flying bomb. It became an important weapon against Britain. The bomb was launched from the ground and flew to its target without a pilot. It could not be aimed very accurately, though. It was designed to frighten the British people rather than strike a specific target. The British quickly learned to identify the loud buzz of the engine of an approaching V1.

At first, the V1 was too fast for antiaircraft guns to hit it. Its speed and height also challenged pilots. However, the British and their allies improved their technology and developed new techniques to fight the V1. Then, in September 1944, Germany launched its first V2 rocket. It flew much higher than the V1. It also traveled faster than the speed of sound, which meant that people could not hear it approaching.

A V2 rocket sits on its launch pad in Cuxhaven, Germany.

"Busy Lizzie"

The V3, or the "Busy Lizzie," was much less effective than the V1 or V2. The V3 launcher was 430 feet (131 m) long and launched ammunition 55 miles (89 km). Designers had hoped for about twice that range.

The V3 that had been intended to target London was destroyed before it could be used. During the Battle of the Bulge, in 1945 in Belgium, German troops used two V3 cannons. Though they fired more than 180 rounds of ammunition, the V3 killed only 10 people.

The Germans planned to launch the V3 rocket from massive underground tunnels such as this one, near the French coast.

Schwerer Gustav means "heavy Gustav" in German.

Adolf Hitler (center) and other German officials inspect the Schwerer Gustav cannon.

Schwerer Gustav

One of the largest guns ever made was Germany's Schwerer Gustav cannon. It could be moved on and fired from railway cars. The gun was originally designed to destroy France's defenses. However, Germany captured France before the gun was ready to use. Even when completed, the cannon was difficult to use. It was so wide that it required side-by-side railways in order to be moved. Also, it took thousands of soldiers to move it and hundreds to fire it.

Radio-Controlled Bombs

From the beginning of the war, airplanes dropped simple bombs from almost directly above the targets. This put the airplane carrying the bomb in danger. To reduce the airplane's risk, German engineers developed radio-controlled bombs such as the Fritz X. This bomb could be dropped far from a target and steered toward it.

Timeline of Weapons in World War II

1940
Spitfires and Hurricanes defend Britain from German bombers during the Battle of Britain.

1941
Soviet troops first use the T-34 tank against the German military.

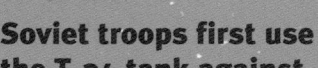

DECEMBER 1941
Japanese bombers attack the U.S. naval base at Pearl Harbor, Hawaii.

The Fritz X was used in particular against ships. During Germany's 1943 invasion of Italy, these bombs damaged several U.S. and other Allied ships. The Allies moved quickly to beat the new technology. They developed radio jammers to confuse the bombs. Long-range cannons were added to battleships. Patrols by airplanes also protected the ships. These changes made radio-controlled bombs such as the Fritz X less effective.

JUNE 1944
Landing craft bring U.S., British, and Canadian troops to Normandy, France, beaches on D-Day.

AUGUST 6, 1945
The first atomic bomb is dropped, on Hiroshima, Japan.

SEPTEMBER 1944
Germany begins using V2 missiles against Britain.

Workers hook an atomic bomb to a tower in New Mexico. It would be raised and then dropped in the world's first atomic bomb test.

The atomic bomb cost the United States about $2 million to develop.

Little Boy and Fat Man

Researchers in the United States had been developing the atomic bomb since 1942. No weapon like it had ever been built. The power of an atomic bomb comes from the energy created when atoms split apart. This creates a shock wave, heat, and **radiation**. The bomb was not ready before Germany surrendered in May 1945. However, as the war against Japan dragged on, U.S. officials decided to use the bomb there.

On August 6, 1945, a U.S. bomber dropped an atomic bomb nicknamed Little Boy on Hiroshima, Japan. Trees were uprooted, buildings were flattened, and 75,000 people died instantly. Thousands more died within days because of radiation poisoning. On August 9, a larger bomb called Fat Man was dropped on Nagasaki, Japan. Japan surrendered. The radiation from both bombs still affects the cities' populations. Though many countries have since developed them, atomic weapons have never been used again. ★

The bomb explosion over Nagasaki sent a mushroom cloud about 60,000 feet (18,288 m) into the air.

43

True Statistics

Average amount of bombs dropped by the United States and its allies each month during World War II: 28,000 tons

Number of U.S. ships sunk by U-boats during World War II: More than 2,800

Percentage of U-boat crew members to survive World War II: About 25

Number of Americans killed during the Pearl Harbor attack: About 2,400

Number of U.S. tanks built during World War II: 89,000

Number of ships and landing craft used during the first day of the Normandy invasion: 5,000

Did you find the truth?

T Some land mines used in World War II launched into the air before exploding.

F British researchers never cracked Germany's secret code during World War II.

Resources

Books

Demuth, Patricia Brennan. *What Was Pearl Harbor?* New York: Grosset & Dunlap, 2013.

Lawton, Clive A. *Hiroshima: The Story of the First Atom Bomb*. Cambridge, MA: Candlewick, 2004.

Stein, Conrad R. *World War II*. New York: Children's Press, 2012.

Important Words

ammunition (am-yuh-NISH-uhn) — things such as bullets or shells that can be fired from weapons

blitzkrieg (BLITZ-kreeg) — war conducted with great speed and force, particularly by massed air and ground forces in close coordination

engineers (en-juh-NEERZ) — people who are specially trained to design and build machines or large structures

radar (RAY-dahr) — a way that ships and planes find solid objects by reflecting radio waves off them and by receiving the reflected waves

radiation (ray-dee-AY-shuhn) — atomic particles that are sent out from a radioactive substance, or a substance whose atoms are breaking down

shrapnel (SHRAP-nuhl) — small pieces of metal thrown out by an exploding shell or bomb

sonar (SOH-nahr) — an instrument used on ships and submarines that sends out underwater sound waves to determine the location of objects and the distance to the bottom

strategy (STAT-i-jee) — a clever plan for winning a military battle or achieving a goal

torpedo (tor-PEE-doh) — an underwater bomb shaped like a tube that explodes when it hits a target, such as a ship

Index

Page numbers in **bold** indicate illustrations

About the Author

Peter Benoit is the author of dozens of books for Children's Press. He has written about American history, ancient civilizations, ecosystems, and more. Peter is also a historical reenactor, occasional tutor, and poet. He is a graduate of Skidmore College, with a degree in mathematics. He lives in Greenwich, New York.